CONQUER CULTURE:
HOW WARRIORS & WINNERS LEAD & SUCCEED

FIELD MANUAL + JOURNAL
By CJ Kirk

Daily Practices. Doctrine Drills. Operational Clarity.

Copyright © 2025 Charles J. (CJ) Kirk

All rights reserved. No part of this publication may be reproduced, distributed, or transmitted in any form or by any means—electronic, mechanical, photocopying, recording, or otherwise—without the prior written permission of the author, except in the case of brief quotations used in reviews, articles, or academic works.

Title: CONQUER CULTURE Field Manual + Journal
Author: Charles J. (CJ) Kirk
Cover Design: Charles J. (CJ) Kirk
Interior Layout: Meredith Kirk Thompson
ISBN: 9798288365652
Printed in the United States of America

First Edition
June 2025

For more information, visit: CONQUERCULTURE.com
To inquire about speaking, bulk orders, or licensing, contact:
CONQUERCULTURE.com

TABLE OF CONTENTS

SECTION I: ORIENTATION — WHAT IS A WARRIOR & WINNER? 1
    1.1 Introduction to the Field Manual
    1.2 Defining a Warrior & Winner
    1.3 Living the Conquer Culture Ethos

SECTION II: GROUND ZERO — ESTABLISHING BASELINE CLARITY 16
    2.1 The Self-Audit Protocol
    2.2 Crafting Your Personal Operating System
    2.3 Establishing Rituals of Recalibration
    2.4 Operational Tools & Templates

SECTION III: PRECURSORS — THE PRECONDITIONS OF GROWTH 39
    3.1 Overview of the Precursors
    3.2 Integrated Practice Pages for Each Precursor
    3.3 Bonus Precursor: Win in the Mind First

SECTION IV: DOCTRINES — THE CORE OPERATING PRINCIPLES 58
    4.1 Overview of Doctrinal Execution
    4.2 Doctrine Practice Pages (19 Total)
    4.3 Monthly Doctrine Integration Cycle
    4.4 Doctrine Groupings by Focus Area

SECTION V: DAILY ENGAGEMENT SYSTEM 86
    5.1 Morning Practice Page
    5.2 Evening Review Page

SECTION VI: WEEKLY RHYTHM RESETS 99
    6.1 Weekly Tactical Review
    6.2 Weekly Targeting & Preparation

SECTION VII: SPECIAL OPERATIONS — HIGH-IMPACT DRILLS   113
    7.1 Situational Challenges & Simulations
    7.2 Sacred Thing Reinforcement Exercises

SECTION VIII: LONG-RANGE VISION & STRATEGIC MAPPING   134
    8.1 90-Day Conquest Plans
    8.2 Annual Leadership Calibration

SECTION IX: CLOSING COMMANDS — LIVING THE CODE   156
    9.1 Your Final Orders
    9.2 Field Manual Commitment Statement

To awaken clarity in a world clouded by deception, to forge the formidable in an age of weakness, and to instill action where passivity reigns.

SECTION I: WHAT IS A WARRIOR & WINNER?

This first section is your reintroduction to who you are—and a reframing of who you are becoming. It's not about hype. It's not about labels. It's about clarity.

Before we can build anything meaningful, we must answer one critical question:

What exactly are we building?

That answer begins with identity. Warriors & Winners are not titles. They're not metaphors. They are identities forged through action, defined by what they serve, and proven in the way they show up—especially under pressure.

You'll begin this manual by stepping into the mirror and taking a hard look. Not at what the world sees. Not at the version you've settled for. But at the high-integrity, high-capacity identity that's been waiting to be built. This section introduces the core distinctions that define a Warrior and a Winner, explores how they operate, and shows you how the CONQUER CULTURE ethos fuses them into one: a person who leads, serves, and sharpens others by how they live.

This isn't theoretical. You'll be asked to name your sacred things. Recalibrate your Ethos. Commit in writing to the journey ahead. The rest of the manual will challenge your discipline and sharpen your execution. But it starts here—with identity.

Section 1.1 Introduction To The Field Manual

This is not just a book. This is not just a journal. This is a field manual—designed to be used, not merely read. You are not here to collect inspiration. You are here to execute. To train. To live with the kind of intentionality and grit that few ever sustain.

The Warriors & Winners Field Manual is your personal operating guide to real transformation—grounded in the CONQUER CULTURE system and built to drive daily action, real-time reflection, and long-term change.

At its core, this manual exists to translate powerful doctrine into embodied practice. It's the hands-on companion to the book, offering a place not just to understand the ideas, but to implement them. And not once, but every single day. This is where insight becomes behavior, and behavior becomes identity. If the main book taught you what's possible, this manual trains you to become it.

The pages ahead are designed for daily engagement. That means you return to them again and again. Each morning, you will take a few moments to align your mind—through breath, through focus, through written reflection. You'll review your current doctrine, declare your intention, and define what execution looks like for that day. This isn't about perfection. It's about repetition. Showing up, again and again, until the work becomes who you are.

In the evening, you will reflect. Not in vague terms like "how did I feel," but with precision—Did you live out your doctrine? Where did you lead? Where did you shrink? What did you conquer? What did you avoid? These questions are the key to growth. They turn experience into mastery.

This manual also contains structured phases of implementation, tied directly to the CONQUER CULTURE method. You'll walk through foundational mindsets, then operationalize the core doctrines, layer in high-performance habits, and finally—if you've done the work—you'll begin to operate with identity-level integration. You'll move from ideas to instincts. From effort to embodiment.

Understand this now: the pages in this manual are not meant to stay clean. They are meant to be filled, marked, circled, scribbled in, rewritten. This is your training ground. Your place to bleed on the page so you can stand up stronger in the world.

The reason this manual exists is simple. Most people don't change because they lack information. They change when that information becomes a daily rhythm. A lived commitment. A habit of thought and action that rewires how they see, how they lead, and how they live. That's what this manual is for.

Wear it out. Use it daily. Use it like your future depends on it—because it does.

Let's jump in.

Section 1.1: Orientation Worksheet

Training Focus: Self-Awareness, Personal Intent, Commitment

1. Why are you here? Why this manual? Why now?

2. What do you hope to gain from fully engaging this process? What are you hungry for? Be specific.

3. When you think of yourself as a Warrior & Winner, what kind of life does that person live?
Describe that future version of you—who they are, how they move, what they stand for.

4. What has historically pulled you off course or kept you from lasting change? Name the resistance. Identify the patterns.

5. Current Mindset Snapshot
Rate yourself on a scale of 1–10 in the following areas:

- Clarity: _____
- Purpose: _____
- Consistency: _____
- Resilience Under Pressure: _____

What needs the most work right now and why?

6. Commitment Declaration

> I will use this manual to train, not just learn.
> I will show up with honesty and hunger.
> I will finish stronger than I started.

Signed: _____

Date: _____

Section 1.2: Defining A Warrior & Winner

Before you can train as a Warrior & Winner, you must understand what that identity demands.

This is not about labels. This is about living from a place of deep alignment—a posture of strength, clarity, and conviction rooted in purpose and action. A Warrior & Winner is not someone who simply endures life or achieves goals. They are a different breed entirely. They are forged through struggle, refined through discipline, and defined by their alignment with truth.

A Warrior is someone who takes up the burden of responsibility with strength and resolve. Warriors move toward resistance, not away from it. They are driven by duty—internal and external. Their lives are marked by courage in the face of fear, composure under pressure, and a willingness to step forward when others shrink back. Warriors don't wait for life to be fair. They fight for what matters.

A Winner, on the other hand, is someone who takes the raw material of life and builds something meaningful with it. They are strategic, persistent, and focused on outcome—not for ego, but for impact. Winners play the long game. They harness pressure and turn it into performance. They know that true winning isn't about applause—it's about legacy. They don't chase trophies; they create results that matter.

Both the Warrior and the Winner live with intention—but their motivations differ slightly.

The Warrior is driven by conviction. The Winner is driven by clarity.

The Warrior will endure for what is right. The Winner will outlast to ensure what is built survives.

The Warrior is forged in willful sacrifice. The Winner is shaped by meaningful pursuit.

Yet at their core, the Warrior and the Winner share the same DNA. They do not drift. They do not defer. They do not operate in mediocrity. And they never blame the external world for their internal state.

When these two roles combine into one identity—when someone lives with the courage of a Warrior and the effectiveness of a Winner—they become something rare. They become someone capable of changing the trajectory of their own life and elevating everyone around them.

This is the optimal Integrated Identity—the fusion of principle and performance, conviction and capability.

The integrated Warrior & Winner lives a life that is both honorable and impactful. Their values aren't theoretical—they're lived. Their wins aren't hollow—they're earned. They don't posture. They don't preach. They model. They execute. They bring presence into every room and precision into every decision. They are grounded in what matters and ruthless in what must be done.

When you see a true Warrior & Winner, you feel it.

They are steady when others break.

They are focused when others scatter.

They are humble, but highly formidable.

And they make the people around them more courageous—because they don't just talk about what's possible. They live it.

You are here to train that identity—that part of you must grow. And it starts now.

You are not here to become someone new. You are here to strip away everything that never belonged to you—the fear, the passivity, the self-doubt, the untrained mind—and to emerge as the Warrior & Winner that has always been there.

This manual is your forge. The pages that follow are your process.

Section 1.2 — Identity Integration Worksheet

Training Focus: Clarity of Self, Role Alignment, Ownership

1. What does the word "Warrior" mean to you?
List the traits, behaviors, mindset, and posture that define this identity.

2. What does the word "Winner" mean to you?
Think beyond trophies. Describe what it looks like to win in life—with depth.

3. Warrior vs. Winner—how do you experience these identities differently? How do they show up in your life right now? How do they sometimes pull in different directions?

4. When have you embodied the Warrior? The Winner? Both?
Briefly recall a time when you fully stepped into each identity—or both at once.

Warrior Moment:

Winner Moment:

Integrated Moment (Both):

5. What parts of your current self are NOT in alignment with either identity?
Name the habits, excuses, fears, or inconsistencies that don't belong.

6. What must happen in the next 30 days for you to walk in full alignment with your Warrior & Winner identity?
Be bold. Be specific. Be honest.

Section 1.3: The Warriors & Winners Ethos

To live and lead as a Warrior & Winner is not merely to adopt a set of behaviors. It is to live from the inside out—with deep, unshakable conviction. And those convictions have a name: ETHOS.

Your ETHOS is not a slogan or a set of inspirational phrases. It is the code embedded within you—the living framework of your values, beliefs, intentions, and guiding principles that must govern your every decision. It is the why behind your actions, the compass when the path is unclear, the anchor when the world tries to pull you in every direction. In a culture increasingly confused about identity, meaning, and direction, ETHOS creates clarity.

The Warrior lives by a code of honor. The Winner lives by a code of execution. But the integrated Warrior & Winner lives by a personal ETHOS forged in both fire and intention—a framework tested in adversity and activated daily.

This ETHOS is not given to you. It must be discovered, forged, committed to and refined. It is born of reflection and choice, of truth faced in the mirror and values chosen in the most sober moments. It is formed when you stop chasing approval and start living from alignment to that ideal.

At its core, your ETHOS answers four foundational questions:

1. Who am I becoming?
2. What do I stand for—regardless of cost?
3. What will I not tolerate—in myself and in the world around me?
4. What am I here to build, protect, or advance?

This is your creed. And if it's not crystal clear, everything else in your life will lack traction.

In this manual, your ETHOS is the first thing you'll develop—and the last thing you'll compromise. You will be guided through reflection prompts, story-based insight, and direct action to craft an ETHOS that reflects your true identity, not your inherited programming. This will not be about what you've been told you should value. It will be about discovering what you must value if you are to live without regret.

Once defined, your ETHOS becomes the lens through which every decision is filtered. Every opportunity is measured against it. Every day is aligned to it. If a behavior, relationship, or pursuit violates your ETHOS—it's out. If it builds toward it—it's in.

It's that simple. And that ruthless.

This is what separates Warriors & Winners from the crowd. Most people wait for clarity to come from the outside. But those who live by ETHOS bring clarity with them. Into every room. Into every challenge. Into every moment.

They don't rely on motivation. They move by the parameters of their mission.

They don't second-guess themselves under pressure. They act from alignment.

They don't get distracted by what others chase. They stay grounded in what matters most.

If you want to live with power, live by ETHOS. If you want to lead with certainty, live by ETHOS. If you want to wake up with energy and go to sleep with peace, live by ETHOS.

Everything in this manual—from your morning rituals to your decision protocols to your legacy goals—will stem from this personal creed.

Because without a clear ETHOS, your strength will fracture under pressure.

But with it, you become unshakable.

In the next section, we will begin shaping your ETHOS—line by line—so that everything that follows isn't just action but aligned action.

When your ETHOS is clear, your life becomes a weapon in the hands of purpose.

Section 1.3: Conquer Culture Ethos Integration

Training Focus: Values Clarity, Personal Alignment, Identity Commitment

---

Sacred Things Inventory

Your Sacred Things are the five anchors that matter most to you—the values, relationships, missions, or convictions you refuse to compromise.

List your Sacred Things below. Be honest. These should stir your soul.

1.
2.
3.
4.
5.

"If I lose these, I lose myself."

Personal Ethos Recalibration

Define what it means to live in alignment with your Sacred Things. Write a personal statement of ethos that can guide your decisions, actions, and leadership.

What does it mean for you to live with integrity, purpose, and alignment?

What specific actions or behaviors that show up in your life would PROVE that you are living by this ethos?

Commitment Page: Your Signature Moment

I commit to living as a Warrior & Winner.

I will not drift. I will not shrink.

I will return to what matters every time I fall.

I will lead, serve, sharpen, and rise.

I will live by my ethos, in full view of the world.

Name (printed): _____

Signature: _____

Today's Date: _____

This is your anchor. Return to it often.

SECTION II — ESTABLISHING BASELINE CLARITY

Before you can lead, perform, or transform—you must get brutally honest about where you are.

Section II is Ground Zero. It's not motivational. It's diagnostic. This is where you pause long enough to map the system you've been operating from so far—your default mode, your personal code, the thoughts, beliefs, and triggers that have been running in the background. Because if you skip this, you'll end up stacking new habits on top of a broken foundation. That's not transformation. That's failure in the making.

This section gives you tools to assess and disrupt the inner mechanics of your operating system—what you believe, how you react, and what drives your patterns. You'll take a Self-Audit. Identify your internal "bad code." Track your triggers. Then you'll craft a new personal operating system designed to support the kind of mindset and life you actually want to build.

You'll also install daily rituals of recalibration—morning and evening structures that create mental order, emotional clarity, and directional power. These aren't soft habits. They are pattern-breaking tools. Use them as directed, and your baseline will start to shift—permanently.

Ground Zero isn't glamorous. It's where excavation happens. But it's also where a new foundation gets poured. The deeper the work, the stronger the future you can build.

Section 2.1: The Self-Audit Protocol

Before a Warrior or Winner can move forward with purpose, they must first confront exactly where they stand. You cannot map your way to dominance or fulfillment if you refuse to mark your current location. This is Ground Zero—the place where clarity begins and self-deception ends.

The Self-Audit Protocol is your first act of honest engagement. Not with others, but with yourself. It's where you learn to see with precision, to identify patterns, to track your defaults, and to prepare your personal operating system for an upgrade. Without this level of introspection, any forward movement is a gamble. With it, every step becomes deliberate.

This protocol consists of three critical components, each designed to reveal the real you—not the projected image or the half-believed narrative, but the truth beneath it all.

Daily Readiness Assessment

Each morning, before the world pulls at your time and attention, you will pause to conduct a simple readiness scan. You'll evaluate your mental, emotional, and physical alignment—your clarity, your presence, your willingness. This is not about grading yourself or guilt. It's about noticing where you are, so you can decide how to move forward. You'll answer prompts like:

- What state am I in today—mentally, emotionally, spiritually?
- What's driving me this morning—intention or inertia?
- Is my breathing shallow or grounded?
- What is my energy rhythm telling me?
- Where is my resistance hiding?

You don't need to be at 100% to win the day. You need to be honest. Warriors are not those who always feel strong—they are those who choose to lead from wherever they are. The Readiness Assessment gives you that leadership choice.

Past Operating System Diagnostic

Our behaviors are not accidents. They are the execution of code—often written in pain, fear, or survival mode. To upgrade your future, you must study your past. This diagnostic helps you trace where your current Personal Operating System came from. What formed it? Who shaped it? What experiences embedded "bad code" into your internal logic?

You'll review:

- What patterns do I keep repeating?
- What self-sabotaging loops have shown up again and again?
- What belief systems were handed to me that I never vetted?
- Who modeled the identity I unconsciously copied?

You will write. You will reflect. You may get angry. But in that process, you will begin to reclaim authorship. This isn't about blame—it's about clarity. And clarity is always power.

Trigger Tracking Worksheet

Until you know what activates you, you'll always be hostage to emotional hijacking. This worksheet trains you to track your primary emotional triggers—the words, situations, postures, tones, and inner dialogues that pull you off-mission. We begin by logging:

- What events cause me to lose control or shift into default?
- What emotions hijack my clarity? (Shame? Pride? Fear? Comparison?)
- What physical responses arise in those moments? (Tension, withdrawal, aggression?)
- What's the story I start telling myself when it happens?

Over time, this log will become a blueprint. You will start seeing patterns—and in those patterns, opportunities. Every emotional trigger is an untrained edge. And every edge, once trained, becomes a weapon.

Together, these three tools—Readiness, Diagnostic, and Trigger Tracking—form the Self-Audit Protocol. It's not a one-time assignment. It's a system for ongoing clarity. You will return to this section again and again, refining your awareness and reclaiming command.

Section 2.1 — The Self-Audit Protocol

Training Focus: Daily Readiness, Internal System Mapping, Pattern Disruption

Daily Readiness Assessment

Use this short self-check to assess your mental, emotional, and spiritual state each morning for the next 7 days. Track your readiness before engaging the day.

Date	Mental (1–10)	Emotional (1–10)	Physical (1–10)	Spiritual (1–10)	Dominant Feeling	Most Pressing Thought

After seven days, review your numbers. Where are you consistently strong? Where are you consistently low? What's the pattern telling you?

Past Operating System Diagnostic

This exercise reveals what core assumptions, habits, and decision-making defaults shaped your past. Use it to name what needs replacing.

What rules or beliefs did you live by over the past 5–10 years that no longer serve you?

Where in your life did you operate on autopilot—repeating behaviors, reactions, or decisions without reflection?

What were the results of those patterns (positive and negative)?

If you continue to operate from that same system, where will it lead you 5 years from now?

Trigger Tracking Worksheet

Identify emotional, environmental, or relational "triggers" that cause you to react in ways that go against your ethos or goals.

Think back over the past two weeks. List five moments where you reacted, avoided, shut down, or overcompensated.

Triggering Event	Emotional Response	Physical Response	Default Behavior	What It Cost You

What pattern do you notice in your responses? What's the deeper story those triggers reveal?

Section 2.2: Crafting Your Personal Operating System

Every person runs on a system—a subconscious framework of beliefs, behaviors, habits, reactions, and interpretations. For most, this system was never chosen. It was inherited, adapted, absorbed, or cobbled together through a thousand unexamined moments. But if you want to live like a Warrior & Winner, you cannot afford to be run by a system you didn't design.

This section is about reclaiming authorship of your internal operating system. It's about choosing what stays, what goes, and what must be rewritten. The world won't hand you clarity or control—you must build it from the inside out. That process begins now.

Core Belief Inventory

Your beliefs dictate your behavior. But most people never stop to ask, "What do I believe? And is it even true?" Before we can engineer a high-performance operating system, we need to audit its most fundamental code: your beliefs.

This isn't about listing nice-sounding values. It's about drilling into what you really believe—what your actions reveal, not just your words. You'll answer:

- What do I believe about my potential?
- What do I believe about struggle, failure, and adversity?
- What do I believe about people, leadership, responsibility, and trust?
- Where did these beliefs come from—and are they serving me or sabotaging me?

You'll explore both "public beliefs" (what you say you believe) and "functional beliefs" (what you actually act on). Wherever there's a gap, a fault line exists. That's where we begin to rewire.

Bad Code Identification

Bad code isn't always obvious. It sounds reasonable. It looks like protection. But in truth, it's a virus—subtle scripts running behind your thoughts that distort your perception, limit your choices, and weaken your power.

These are thoughts like:

- "I'm not enough."
- "If I fail, it means I am a failure."
- "I need to prove my worth daily."

This step is about surfacing those lines of code—identifying where they live, when they activate, and how they shape your operating system. You'll track:

- What internal narratives trigger hesitation or shame?
- What patterns emerge when I face risk, conflict, or judgment?
- What protective strategies do I run on autopilot—and what do they cost me?

The goal isn't to condemn yourself. It's to see clearly. Because what you can see, you can change.

Default Mode to Deliberate Mode Mapping

Once you've identified your old code, the question becomes: what system do you want to run now?

This step is about designing an updated operating system—consciously, deliberately, and in alignment with your ETHOS and Sacred Things. You will map out the shift from your old "default mode" to your new "deliberate mode" in key domains:

- Decision-making under pressure
- Handling failure or setbacks
- Navigating relationships and leadership
- Responding to challenge, resistance, or temptation

You will script:

- What would my new internal dialogue sound like in a moment of doubt?
- What physical posture or breath pattern will anchor my deliberate mode?
- What phrase, image, or trigger can I use to shift from reaction to intention?

Then you will practice this new mode—repeatedly, daily, and with full awareness. You're not just rewriting thoughts. You're reprogramming action. Your nervous system, your attention, your habits, your language. Everything.

You're building a new system that no longer runs on fear, avoidance, or old pain. You're replacing it with precision, power, and purpose.

And once that system is live—your life will reflect it. Every choice, every conversation, every challenge will become a proving ground for the new identity you are now living into.

This is how transformation sticks.

Not by inspiration.

By installation.

And it starts with crafting the code that will run your next chapter.

Section 2.2 — Crafting Your Personal Operating System

Training Focus: Belief Inventory, Bad Code Replacement, Identity Alignment

---

Core Belief Inventory

Start by identifying the foundational beliefs that have shaped your identity and behavior. Then evaluate if they are rooted in truth—or in outdated programming.

1. What do you believe about yourself? (Finish the sentence: "I am…")

2. What do you believe about others and the world around you? (Finish the sentence: "People are…" and "Life is…")

3. Where did these beliefs come from? Who or what shaped them?

4. Which of these beliefs have consistently empowered you?

5. Which beliefs have limited you or led you into cycles you regret?

Bad Code Identification

Bad code is corrupted belief or behavior logic—stories, assumptions, or learned responses that once helped you survive but now sabotage you.

List 3–5 internal messages, narratives, or instincts you now recognize as "bad code."

Choose one bad code pattern above. Now rewrite it using truth-based, empowering language that reflects your Ethos.

Old Code:

New Operating Belief:

Default Mode to Deliberate Mode Mapping

Map out your default responses—and replace them with deliberate, Ethos-aligned alternatives. Identify three real-life scenarios where you tend to react in your default mode. Then design a new, deliberate response.

Situation	Default Mode Response	Internal Story	Deliberate Response	Behavior Shift

What would change in your life if you showed up this way consistently? What relationships, habits, or outcomes would begin to shift?

Section 2.3: Establishing Rituals of Recalibration

When the stakes are high and the noise of life is relentless, clarity becomes a competitive advantage—and ritual becomes your reset button. The world doesn't slow down. The demands don't stop. That's why you must train yourself to pause on purpose, recalibrate, and re-engage from a place of power and alignment.

This subsection is about constructing the daily and weekly rhythms that keep you grounded, focused, and intentional. These are not filler routines or productivity hacks. These are recalibration rituals—deliberate, repeatable frameworks that realign your internal operating system with your Warrior & Winner identity.

Done once, they center you. Done daily, they change you.

Morning Practice Template

How you begin your day sets the tone for how you interpret and respond to everything that follows. Morning is not just a time slot. It is your first battlefield. It's where you claim your frequency, recalibrate your state, and declare who you will be before the world has a chance to tell you otherwise.

Your morning ritual includes:

- Breath Activation – Begin with 3–5 minutes of breath work. Choose a method: box breathing, tactical inhale-exhale, or breath-hold work. This is how you engage presence and break the inertia of sleep.
- One True Priority – Identify the single, non-negotiable outcome that must be accomplished to move your mission forward today.
- Ethos Check-In – Read your Personal ETHOS or Sacred Things aloud. Re-anchor your identity.
- Doctrine of the Day – Choose one Warrior & Winner Doctrine to engage. Write it. Speak it. Reflect on how you will live it.

- Sacred Question – Ask one question to stir depth: "Where will I show courage today?" "Where will I lead when it's easier to follow?" "What am I avoiding that must be faced?"

The goal isn't complexity. It's calibration. This practice may take 10–15 minutes, but the alignment it creates will alter every hour that follows.

Evening Review Template

Most people go to sleep with mental clutter, emotional residue, and untapped insight sitting in their system. Warriors & Winners do not drift into sleep. They review, reflect, and reset.

The evening ritual includes:

- Action Audit – What did I do today that honored my values, my goals, and my identity? What did I avoid or neglect?
- Resistance Debrief – When and where did resistance show up today? How did I respond? What did it teach me?
- Micro-Win Recognition – What one moment—no matter how small—was a win today? Build the habit of seeing your progress.
- Integrity Score (1–10) – Rate yourself honestly. Did you live today aligned with your Ethos and Doctrine? Not to judge—only to track.
- Noticing & Adjustments – What stood out? What will I carry forward into tomorrow with greater precision?

The goal of the evening ritual is not perfection. It's pattern recognition. What gets tracked gets trained. And what gets trained becomes who you are.

Weekly Rhythm Reset Format

Each week is a campaign—a mission to advance. But without regular pause and recalibration, weeks blur into months, and momentum dissolves into chaos.

The Weekly Rhythm Reset is your mission brief and recalibration ritual all in one. It includes:

- Review the Week Behind – Where did I advance? Where did I fall short? What patterns are emerging in my thought, execution, and emotion?
- Doctrine Integration Log – Which doctrines did I engage? How did I apply them? Where did I miss the mark?
- Precursor Integration – How often and how deeply did I engage my Growth Precursors? Where do I need more intentionality?
- Leadership Moments – Where did I lead from the front? Where did I retreat? What must be adjusted?
- Mission Reset – What is my mission for the week ahead? What is the priority? Where is the pressure point?

This weekly review isn't just for tracking performance. It's for ensuring that your rhythm doesn't get hijacked by urgency, emotion, or drift. It's your chance to stay on purpose, stay on pattern, and stay on point.

These rituals aren't glamorous. They aren't public. But they are sacred.

They are the quiet disciplines that reforge you into the kind of man or woman who doesn't just start strong—but finishes stronger.

Warriors & Winners don't wait to recalibrate when life falls apart. They recalibrate every day—on purpose.

So set your ritual. Protect it fiercely. And let it protect your clarity in return.

Section 2.3 — Establishing Rituals of Recalibration

Training Focus: Morning Practice, Evening Review, Weekly Reset

Morning Practice Template

Use this each morning to center your mind, prime your day, and align with your Warrior & Winner ethos.

Date: _____

Wake Time: _____

Sleep Quality (1–10): _____

Breath Practice (circle one):
Box | 4–7–8 | Tactical | Other: _____

Sacred Thing I Will Honor Today:

Today's One True Priority:

Doctrine of the Day:

Intentional Statement (How will I show up?):

Warrior Question of the Day (e.g., Where will I lead today? What will I do differently?):

Evening Review Template

Use this each night to close the loop on your day, record lessons, and reinforce your identity.

Date: _____

Summary of Actions Taken Toward My Priority:

Where I Led Well Today:

Where I Drifted or Reacted:

Resistance Faced & How I Responded:

Micro-Win of the Day (small win worth noting):

Integrity Check (1–10): _____

What pulled me down or lifted me up today?

Reset Intention for Tomorrow:

Weekly Rhythm Reset Format (Use at the end of each week)

This reset helps you recalibrate, refocus, and recommit. Do this every 7 days.

Week #: _____ | Date Range: _____ to _____

Biggest Win of the Week:

Biggest Resistance or Regression:

Most Activated Doctrine or Precursor:

Score Your Week (1–10): _____ | Why that score?

What Needs Recalibration or Reinforcement?

Top Focus or Micro-Goal for Next Week:

Doctrine I Will Train Intentionally:

Sacred Thing That Must Be Honored Next Week:

SECTION III — PRECURSORS: THE PRECONDITIONS OF GROWTH

Before you master any doctrine, build any system, or lead anyone else—you must first become coachable. And that starts with embracing the precursors.

Precursors are the inner attitudes and baseline mental states that make transformation possible. They aren't optional. They're prerequisites. Just like a fighter needs flexibility before strength, or an entrepreneur needs clarity before strategy, you need these mental and emotional orientations before you can apply the deeper work in this manual.

This section will walk you through each precursor—explaining why it matters, how to train it, and how to measure your integration over time. These aren't philosophical musings. They're performance prerequisites. The precursors challenge your ego. They dismantle unproductive pride. They pull you out of stagnation and into a mode where you're actually ready to receive, respond, and evolve.

Each precursor has a practice page built for real engagement. You'll reflect. You'll track your progress. You'll take bold action in small ways that recalibrate your internal compass. And you'll begin to notice—your default reactivity changes, your self-awareness sharpens, and your emotional stamina expands.

Without these precursors, doctrine feels like pressure. With them, doctrine becomes power.

Section 3.1: Overview of the Precursors

Before mastery, there must be movement. Before discipline, desire. Before doctrine can be applied, something deeper must take root—a posture, a mindset, a readiness to grow. These are the Growth Precursors.

The precursors are not strategies or tactics. They are preconditions—the internal shifts required before external change is possible. They are the mental, emotional, and spiritual orientations that must be activated before a Warrior & Winner can fully engage the doctrines that follow.

This section of the Field Manual exists to help you implement them—not just to understand, but to install. Because if you miss the precursors, you'll fumble the disciplines. You'll encounter the doctrines with shallow soil. The result will be surface-level action, not deep transformation.

We don't want that. You don't want that. So, let's get clear on what this is—and how to use it.

What They Are & Why They Matter

Each precursor operates like a switch—a recalibration of posture that unlocks your capacity to grow. They exist to eliminate what blocks momentum before it starts. To disarm the internal resistance that would otherwise delay, dilute, or destroy your progress.

- Empty the Cup reminds you to unlearn before you learn.
- Get Underway teaches that nothing changes until you move.
- Suspend Disbelief invites you to question what you've accepted as immovable.
- Eat the Elephant reframes overwhelming tasks into digestible victories.
- Practice Non-Judgment opens the door to progress without self-sabotage.
- Prove It to Yourself shifts your power source from belief to action.
- Guard Your Thoughts instills vigilance over your inner state.

- Take Calculated Risks gives you permission to move with courage, not recklessness.

These are not passive ideas. Each one is a primer—a mechanism designed to prepare the ground for everything else this manual will ask of you.

Without the precursors, doctrine feels forced. With them, it flows.

How to Engage Them Daily

This Field Manual does not exist for inspiration. It exists for implementation.

So here is how you'll engage the precursors in your daily rhythm:

Each week, you will focus on one precursor. One idea. One internal shift. You will revisit it every morning in your Daily Practice Page and reflect on it each night in your Evening Review.

You will write about it, live into it, and track its influence on your decisions, your thoughts, and your actions.

You are not here to master all eight at once. You are here to embody one at a time—over and over—until it stops being something you do and starts being something you are.

When you've cycled through all eight, you'll begin again. Why? Because precursors aren't checklists. They're calibrators. You don't graduate from them. You grow deeper into them.

You'll know a precursor is working when it shows up in your real life—when your default reactions start changing. When your excuses begin to feel weak in the face of what you now know. When your actions reflect not just who you want to be, but who you are actively becoming.

Each spread in the next section will walk you through the practice for a single precursor.

Read it. Sit with it. Live it.

Because in this work, it's not how much you know. It's how deeply you engage.

Section 3.1 — Overview of the Precursors

Training Focus: Awareness, Activation, and Alignment

> "The mind is the arena of transformation. The precursors are the first strike."

The Growth Precursors are not warm-ups. They are the ignition sequence. These are not mere suggestions to "think about." Each one is a trigger for change—an internal shift that clears space, initiates movement, and exposes the patterns that must be upgraded if you're going to live as a Warrior & Winner.

This is your starting ground. You are not here to feel good. You are here to become different.

REFLECT: Your Current Baseline with Growth

Answer the following to anchor your awareness before engaging the precursor practices.

What has consistently blocked your growth in the past?

What internal stories, attitudes, or beliefs have kept you stuck?

What would real change feel like in your life? How would you notice it taking root?

CLARIFY: What Precursor Practice Means to You

Use the space below to engage intentionally with the Precursor section. This sets the tone for the practice pages that follow.

What does it mean to you to "prepare for growth" intentionally, rather than waiting for it to happen?

Which of the following do you sense will be your greatest growth edge? (circle or underline):

Empty Your Cup | Suspend Disbelief | Eat the Elephant | Practice Non-Judgment
Prove It to Yourself | Guard Your Thoughts | Take Calculated Risks | Underway - Why that one? What discomfort does it challenge in you?

REINFORCE: Weekly Precursor Practice Commitment

Use this as a weekly re-commitment space to ensure your growth isn't passive but deliberate.

Precursor I Will Practice This Week:

How I Will Engage It Daily:

Obstacle I Might Face / Pattern That Might Resist It:

How I Will Interrupt the Resistance:

What Would Success Look Like by Week's End?

Section 3.2: Integrated Practice Pages for Each Precursor

You've now been introduced to what the precursors are and why they matter. But understanding them conceptually isn't the mission. Living them is. That's why this section is structured to help you make each precursor real—visceral, visible, and active in your daily experience.

Each of the following spreads is dedicated to one precursor.

This isn't just journaling. This is integration.

The goal here is to make each precursor a functional part of your mindset and operating system. These pages are designed to slow you down, guide your focus, and give you a place to measure the quality of your engagement—not to track perfection, but to track attention and presence.

Every week, you'll select one precursor and use the dedicated practice spread to deepen its influence in your life. The rhythm is simple but profound: reflect, plan, execute, and capture what you notice.

Let's break down how to use each part of the practice spread:

1. Reflection Prompts
At the top of each spread, you'll find 2–3 tailored reflection questions. These are not philosophical musings—they're working prompts. Use them to inspect your current beliefs and behaviors in light of the precursor. Challenge yourself to answer honestly, not optimistically. If the precursor is "Prove It to Yourself," you might be asked:

- Where am I relying on belief instead of evidence?
- What actions this week would serve as undeniable proof of growth?

Your answers don't need to be elegant—they need to be real. Don't write for the page. Write for the fight you're in.

---

2. Action Plan Fields

Below the reflections, you'll define exactly how you intend to live out this precursor over the next seven days. Choose one or two actionable behaviors, commitments, or mindset shifts that align with the week's focus. For example:

- For "Guard Your Thoughts," you might commit to redirecting every negative self-statement in real time and recording the experience.
- For "Empty the Cup," you might target one area of your life where you'll deliberately unlearn something that's no longer useful.

Write down your plan. Keep it simple. Then treat it like a mission order.

3. Weekly Self-Scoring (1–10 Scale)

Each practice spread includes a 1–10 scale to evaluate how consistently and courageously you lived into the precursor over the course of the week. This isn't about performance—it's about pattern recognition. You're not scoring whether the week was "good" or "bad." You're scoring how fully you engaged.

Track it. Own it. Adjust accordingly.

4. Insights & Noticing Log

At the bottom of the spread is space to capture what you saw, felt, and learned throughout the week. This could be a breakthrough, a recurring resistance, a new awareness, or even a failure you now recognize more clearly. These insights are gold—each one is a feedback signal from the system of your life.

Write them down. Study them. They will teach you exactly where your next growth edge lives.

Important Note: Cycle, Don't Sprint

You don't need to "master" each precursor in a single week. You need to build a relationship with it. Most readers will benefit from cycling through these pages every 8–10 weeks, returning to each precursor with deeper perspective and new life context.

Each cycle reveals more. Each cycle strips away something untrue and reinforces something essential.

By tracking your reflections, action plans, scores, and noticing over time, you'll begin to map your personal transformation with precision. You'll see exactly how you're evolving—and exactly what needs more attention.

This is where precursors become permanent.

This is where growth becomes inevitable.

Start now. Choose your first precursor. Open the page. Begin the work. And let that work shape the person you are becoming—one deliberate week at a time.

Precursor Workbook

The precursors are not optional. They are the preconditions of growth—mental, emotional, and spiritual postures that must be established before any high-performance doctrine or advanced execution strategy can take root. Without them, the doctrines that follow will be misunderstood, misapplied, or quickly abandoned when resistance shows up. These precursors are the hidden foundations that Warriors & Winners rely on—often unconsciously—as their baseline operating standard. But now, you will engage them consciously and deliberately.

This section of the manual is your working laboratory. Each precursor will challenge you to reflect, respond, and take aligned action. Don't skim. Don't just agree with the ideas. Instead, meet each one with full presence. Reflect in writing. Score yourself honestly. Extract insight. Then translate that insight into action.

You are not here to nod in agreement.
You are here to rewire your operating system.

Precursor #1: Empty Your Cup

Reflection Prompt:
What assumptions, past failures, or experiences might prevent me from fully engaging in this process today?

Daily Action Commitment:
Today, I will let go of:

Self-Rating (1–10): _____
Insights & Noticing:

Precursor #2: Underway is the Only Way

Reflection Prompt:

Where am I over-planning or procrastinating when I should be moving?

Daily Action Commitment:

One thing I will start now, even if imperfect:

Self-Rating (1–10): _____

Insights & Noticing:

Precursor #3: Suspend Disbelief

Reflection Prompt:
What belief about myself or the world might I need to suspend to move forward?

Daily Action Commitment:
Today, I will act "as if" the following is true:

Self-Rating (1–10): _____
Insights & Noticing:

Precursor #4: Eat the Elephant

Reflection Prompt:
What goal or challenge seems overwhelming right now?

Daily Action Commitment:
What is one bite-sized action I will take today?

Self-Rating (1–10): _____
Insights & Noticing:

Precursor #5: Practice Non-Judgment

Reflection Prompt:

Where am I judging myself or this process instead of observing and adjusting?

Daily Action Commitment:

Today, I will observe the following without judgment:

Self-Rating (1–10): _____

Insights & Noticing:

Precursor #6: Prove It to Yourself

Reflection Prompt:
What truth do I need to test through action rather than assumption?

Daily Action Commitment:
What one thing will I do today to verify that I'm growing?

Self-Rating (1–10): _____
Insights & Noticing:

Precursor #7: Guard Your Thoughts

Reflection Prompt:

What thoughts today have been unproductive, negative, or misaligned with my goals?

Daily Action Commitment:

What thought pattern will I interrupt or replace today?

Self-Rating (1–10): _____

Insights & Noticing:

Precursor #8: Take Calculated Risks

Reflection Prompt:
What am I avoiding because of fear, not logic?

Daily Action Commitment:
What risk will I take today that aligns with my purpose and values?

Self-Rating (1–10): _____
Insights & Noticing:

Bonus Precursor: Win in the Mind

Reflection Prompt:

Where in my life do I try to win with effort before I've won with mindset?

Daily Action Commitment:

How will I mentally rehearse victory before pressure shows up today?

Self-Rating (1–10): _____

Insights & Noticing:

SECTION IV — DOCTRINES: THE CORE OPERATING PRINCIPLES

This is the heart of the system.

If the precursors are the roots, the doctrines are the spine—unyielding, essential, and governing every move you make. These principles are not just beliefs; they are behavioral codes. Each doctrine has been field-tested in the lives of Warriors & Winners across industries, environments, and high-pressure situations. These aren't theories. They are operational truths—short enough to remember, deep enough to guide, sharp enough to cut through confusion.

The doctrines are broken into three primary focus areas: Decisive Action, Strategic Mastery, and Leading with Purpose. Each one carries a distinct internal shift and a visible behavioral pattern. When trained together, they form a new personal operating system—one that is resilient, intentional, and equipped for sustained performance under pressure.

This section is where you build muscle memory for the values you say you hold. Every doctrine comes with a review, an application challenge, and space to reflect on your daily alignment. These are not journal prompts for passive introspection. They are calibration tools—designed to hold you accountable, push your edge, and reveal gaps between what you believe and how you behave.

This is the work that builds identity. This is where discipline becomes instinct.

Train each doctrine until it's embedded in how you move, how you decide, and how you lead.

Section 4.1: Overview of Doctrinal Execution

Doctrines are not motivational statements or vague ideas. They are tested truths—operating principles forged in pressure, proven in execution, and built to rewire your life. In the Warriors & Winners system, doctrines represent the code that replaces the bad programming of your old default. They are not just beliefs. They are behavioral imperatives.

Every doctrine in this field manual was chosen because it works. These are the principles that high performers, elite warriors, exceptional leaders, and resilient men and women live by—whether they've ever named them or not. You now have a clear set of these tools, spelled out and ready for integration.

But knowing the doctrines isn't enough. You must cycle them.

And more importantly, you must train them.

How to Cycle Doctrines Weekly

Each week, you will select one doctrine to focus on. That doctrine will become your lens for daily action and reflection. For seven days, you'll study it, live it, track it, and let it expose where you drift or hold back. The goal is to internalize one principle at a time until it moves from insight to instinct.

Each week's cycle will follow a pattern:

1. Day 1: Doctrine Reset – Read the doctrine summary, highlight the value, opportunity, and quality required. Anchor it in your journal. Define what living this doctrine looks like in your context right now.
2. Days 2–6: Daily Check-Ins – In your Daily Practice Pages, log your intentional application. Look for where the doctrine was present in your behavior—and where it wasn't. Capture noticing.

3. Day 7: Doctrine Reflection – Use the weekly reflection space to answer the challenge questions: Where did I live this? Where did I leave this? What's shifting? What needs more work?

After 3–4 weeks of individual doctrine practice, you will enter a rotation phase where you group doctrines in threes, intensifying your load and simulating real-life overlap.

Doctrine Groupings by Focus Area

To aid your practice, doctrines are organized into four primary focus areas. You can train them in sequence, or you can cycle through groupings based on your current needs. Each grouping sharpens a different dimension of the Warrior & Winner operating system.

1. Mental Mastery
    - Win in the Mind First
    - Fine-Tune Your Frequency (FIVR)
    - Prove It to Yourself
    - Failure is Necessary
2. Decisive Action
    - The 5-Minute Rule
    - Fix Your Problem
    - Closest Weapon, Nearest Target
    - Retzev (Continuous Attack)
3. Strategic Execution
    - Prioritize, Simplify, Organize
    - Master the OODA Loop
    - Skip to the End
    - Rent to Own
    - Speed & Leverage at 90 Degrees
4. Leadership & Legacy
    - Lead from the Front

- Constant Directional Pressure (CDP)
- Permanent Growth from Sustainable Qualities
- Potential, Principles & Passion = Meaning
- Perfection is Not Required

These groupings allow you to train a full bandwidth of capability—starting with mindset, moving into action, then strategy, then purpose and leadership. If you're unsure where to begin, start with Mental Mastery. If you're under pressure or actively leading others, move to Decisive Action or Leadership & Legacy.

The key is to move with intention. Let each doctrine work on you. Track what it disrupts, what it sharpens, what it reveals. And above all, live it in real-time—not in theory, not in abstraction, but in how you show up each day.

This is the heart of the field manual. Doctrine not just as content—but as compass, as call, as code.

Section 4.2: Doctrine Practice Pages

This section is where theory is turned into traction—where you don't just revisit the doctrines, you apply them in real time, against the pressure and unpredictability of your actual life. Each of these pages is designed to help you bring a specific doctrine into focus, move it from concept to conduct, and evaluate your execution day by day.

Every doctrine in this manual gets its own dedicated practice spread—an entire workspace for living that truth with clarity, intention, and discipline.

You will begin each spread by reviewing the doctrine at hand—what it means, why it matters, and what success looks like when that principle is fully lived. You'll have space to summarize the doctrine in your own words, sharpening your understanding and personalizing its application.

Each day, you'll identify how that doctrine shows up in your world:

- Where is this principle needed most right now?
- What obstacles are testing it?
- What opportunities can be won by living it well?

Then comes the Daily Application Check-In. This isn't a checkbox. It's an accountability window. You'll capture the moment where you showed up aligned—or the moment where you didn't. You'll build a feedback loop of clarity: where did I lead from the front today? Where did I drift? What am I learning about how this doctrine works under pressure?

At the end of each week, you'll complete the Challenge & Reflection prompts. These are deeper assessments—not just whether you "did the thing," but what you discovered about yourself while doing it. You'll be asked:

- Where did I live this doctrine under real pressure?
- Where did I leave it behind when it mattered?
- What did I learn about my default patterns?
- What specific adjustments must I make to align more fully?

These questions are your recalibration tools. They're meant to keep you honest, focused, and free from the illusion of progress without actual performance.

Some doctrines will hit hard. Others will require repeated exposure. That's why this format allows you to cycle through again and again over time. You don't master a doctrine in a week. You build fluency. You test it against life. You sharpen it in the crucible of daily decisions.

By journaling through these pages, you're not simply reflecting—you're rewiring. You're not collecting ideas—you're building instincts. And that's the goal of this section: to form a personal, behavioral relationship with each doctrine so that your nervous system, not just your intellect, knows what to do when pressure shows up.

This is how you build unshakable alignment. One doctrine at a time. One week at a time. One honest reflection at a time.

Turn the page. Begin the next spread. Live the doctrine. Then come back and refine.

Doctrine Subset 1 — Clarify & Command Your Operating System

Doctrines 1–4: Prioritize / Simplify / Organize | Fine-Tune Your Frequency | Failure is Necessary | The 5-Minute Rule

---

Doctrine #1: Prioritize, Simplify, Organize

Key Principle:
Complexity kills clarity. Power is wasted when your life, thoughts, or systems are scattered. Prioritize what matters most, simplify the path forward, and organize your world to match your mission.

Daily Application Practice:

- What must get done today to move my mission forward?
- What needs to be removed, delayed, or simplified?
- Where is disorganization leaking energy from my system?

One True Priority (Today):

Declutter Commitment (Today):

Reflection:
Where did clarity emerge after simplification? Where did chaos still rule?

Doctrine #2: Fine-Tune Your Frequency (FIVR)

Key Principle:
Your inner state dictates your outer performance. Fine-tuning your Frequency, Intensity, Velocity, and Rhythm (FIVR) determines whether you operate in alignment or agitation.

FIVR Self-Check (circle):
Frequency (Am I present enough?): Low / Medium / High
Intensity (Am I over/under-engaged?): Low / Medium / High
Velocity (Am I rushing or dragging?): Low / Medium / High
Rhythm (Am I in sync with my environment?): Off / In Flow

Frequency Reset Practice (Breath, Pause, Anchor):
What specific tool will I use today to recalibrate if I drift?

Noticing:
What internal shift changed my external outcome today?

Doctrine #3: Failure is Necessary

Key Principle:
Failure isn't just acceptable—it's essential. It's the friction that forges mastery. Those who avoid it remain weak. Those who embrace it become formidable.

Micro-Failure Reflection (Today):
Where did I fall short or get resistance?

Reframe It:
What did I learn or gain from that failure?

Conviction Commitment:
How will I attack again with more wisdom tomorrow?

Doctrine #4: The 5-Minute Rule

Key Principle:
Over-celebration and over-suffering both rob you of momentum. Process emotion. Then move. Momentum is the antidote to stagnation.

Victory / Failure Trigger (Today):
What moment tried to trap me emotionally today?

Did I Move in 5 Minutes or Less?
Yes / No
If not, what did I do instead?

Next Time Protocol:
If it happens again, how will I re-engage?

Doctrine Subset 2 — Take Bold, Decisive Action

Doctrines 5–8: Fix Your Problem | Cause Pain, Break Balance, Take Control | Closest Weapon, Nearest Target | Retzev (Continuous Attack)

Doctrine #5: Fix Your Problem

Key Principle:
Warriors & Winners don't outsource problems—they own and fix them. They act with what they have, adapt on the fly, and train for chaos, not comfort.

Today's Problem (Be Specific):

Action Taken (Don't wait, move):

Adaptability Reflection:
What mindset or tool helped me step forward?
What resistance did I overcome?

Doctrine #6: Cause Pain, Break Balance, Take Control

Key Principle:
Disruption is a weapon. Whether in combat, business, or life, those who win know when and where to break the pattern—physical, psychological, or emotional.

Targeted Disruption (Today):
Where did I apply force or influence to create advantage?

Control Reclaimed:
How did I shift power, reframe a moment, or stabilize a chaotic environment?

Intention Check:
Was this disruption tactical or emotional?
What was the purpose?

Doctrine #7: Closest Weapon, Nearest Target

Key Principle:
Use what you have, now. The most effective action is always the one you can execute immediately. Waiting for ideal conditions is a form of surrender.

Current Challenge:

Closest Weapon (Tool, Insight, Skill, Connection):

Nearest Target (What can I affect right now?):

Action Taken (No delay):

Doctrine #8: Retzev — Continuous Attack

Key Principle:
Momentum wins. Whether in movement, conversation, or action, the seamless transition between engagements keeps you ahead of resistance, distraction, and delay.

Where Did I Move Forward Relentlessly Today?
Describe a moment when you continued, even after discomfort hit:

Where Did I Stall or Pause Without Cause?
What stopped the chain? What interruption disrupted flow?

Momentum Rebuild Commitment (for Tomorrow):
What's one sequence I will execute without pause?

Doctrine Subset 3 — Develop Strategic Mastery

Doctrines 9–12: Speed & Leverage at 90 Degrees | Master the OODA Loop | Skip to the End | Rent to Own

---

Doctrine #9: Speed & Leverage at 90 Degrees

Key Principle:
Winning doesn't always require more effort—it requires better angles. Strategic placement of pressure creates exponential force.

Today's Misalignment (Where I Was Wasting Energy):

Course Correction:
Where did I identify and apply force at the right angle for maximum result?

Insight:
What opportunity appeared once I stopped pushing directly and changed the angle?

Doctrine #10: Master the OODA Loop

Key Principle:
Observe. Orient. Decide. Act. Speed and clarity in this cycle is how you take ground while others hesitate.

Today's Scenario:
Describe a situation where you needed to think and act quickly:

Where I Slowed the Loop: Where did I hesitate, over-analyze, or act too late?

Loop Discipline (What I Did Well):
What did I observe early? How did I orient with clarity?
What helped me decide and act with confidence?

Doctrine #11: Skip to the End

Key Principle:
Anticipation shortens the road. When you know the likely conclusion, you can reverse-engineer the steps that get you there and eliminate wasted motion.

Today's Vision:
What outcome did I clearly define?

Backwards Mapping (Steps I Saw and Executed in Reverse):

Where I Hesitated:
Where did I "stay in the weeds" instead of jumping ahead with clarity?

Doctrine #12: Rent to Own

Key Principle:
You don't own what you don't embody. Warriors & Winners integrate knowledge through repetition, reflection, and real-world application.

Lesson or Skill I Am "Renting" But Haven't Fully Owned Yet:

Today's Ownership Action (Put It Into Practice):
What did I do with it today? Where did I apply it under pressure?

Proof of Integration:
What feedback, result, or internal shift showed me I'm starting to own this?

Doctrine Subset 4 — Lead with Purpose

Doctrines 13–16: Constant Directional Pressure | Find & Leverage Your Natural Rhythm | Lead from the Front | Potential, Principles & Passion = Meaning

Doctrine #13: Constant Directional Pressure (CDP)

Key Principle:
Progress is the product of unrelenting, intentional force over time. Pressure must not only be constant—it must be intelligently directed.

Where I Applied CDP Today (and Why It Mattered):

Break in Pressure:
Where did I let off the gas? What was the cost?

Recommitment Point:
Where must I resume sustained pressure with focus?

Doctrine #14: Find & Leverage Your Natural Rhythm

Key Principle:
You are built for flow. When you align your actions with your own peak performance rhythm—mental, emotional, physical—you multiply output and preserve energy.

Peak Energy Window Noticed Today:
When was I most clear, most energized, or most effective?

Where I Worked Against My Rhythm:

One Adjustment for Tomorrow (Rhythm-Driven):

Doctrine #15: Lead from the Front

Key Principle:
People follow courage, not commands. The most powerful form of leadership is visible example under pressure.

Where I Led by Example Today:

Where I Drifted or Played Small (Missed Opportunity to Lead):

Leadership Pulse Check:
What did others see in me today?

Doctrine #16: Potential, Principles & Passion Yields Meaning

Key Principle:
Sustainable success is built at the intersection of who you are (potential), what you stand for (principles), and what drives you (passion).

Today's Alignment Assessment:
Where did I operate in alignment with all three?

Where I Felt Out of Sync:
What was missing—potential, principle, or passion?

Reconnection Action:
What one action will realign me tomorrow?

Doctrine #17: Become a Master of Time

Key Principle:
Later is a lie. Warriors & Winners don't wait for perfect conditions—they take control of time by acting with urgency and clarity in the now. Time is a battlefield. Those who hesitate are defeated by drift. Those who act decisively control outcomes and momentum.

Precision Prompt – Real Time Focus:
Where did I move today without delay, taking fast and purposeful action?

Decision Check – Moment of Delay:
What did I put off today that should have been done in real time?

Reclaiming the Clock:
What action can I take tomorrow—immediately and without waiting—that will signal I've mastered the moment?

Doctrine #18: Permanent Growth Comes from Sustainable Qualities

Key Principle:
Success that lasts is built on strength that lasts. Warriors & Winners don't chase growth through external metrics alone—they cultivate purpose, ownership, meaning, and internal congruence. These are the sustainable forces that never collapse under pressure.

Integrity Check – Source of Power Today:
Where did I operate today from purpose, meaning, or long-term vision?

Sustainability Gauge – Internal vs External Fuel:
Did I finish the day more grounded or more depleted?

Root Reinforcement:
What core quality must I deepen to ensure tomorrow's growth is lasting?

Doctrine #19: Perfection is Not Required

Key Principle:
Perfection is the enemy of progress. Warriors & Winners understand that forward motion beats flawless planning. They don't let fear dress itself in high standards. They act, adapt, and repeat—because consistent execution builds greatness.

Today's Imperfect Action:
What did I do today even though it wasn't perfect?

Perfection Trap – Where I Stalled:
Where did perfectionism slow me down, delay action, or create frustration?

Bias Toward Action Commitment:
What will I do tomorrow without over-polishing, over-editing, or overthinking?

Section 4.3: Monthly Doctrine Integration Cycle

True transformation isn't created through exposure—it's forged through repetition. You cannot simply read a doctrine once, nod in agreement, and expect your life to shift. The doctrines outlined in this system must be revisited, rehearsed, and rotated into your lived experience consistently over time. The Monthly Doctrine Integration Cycle exists to structure that repetition into a form you can commit to, track, and grow from.

Overview:
Each month, you will select three doctrines to intentionally integrate into your personal operating system. These are not passive themes to reflect on—they are active lenses through which you will view decisions, confront challenges, and shape your behavior in the real world. Think of them as software updates to your identity. They will run in the background of every significant choice you make.

How to Begin the Monthly Cycle:

1. Doctrine Selection:
   At the start of each new month, choose three doctrines. Don't pick randomly. Instead, reflect on the areas where you feel tension, stagnation, or opportunity. Which doctrines directly confront your current limitations? Which ones feel uncomfortable, convicting, or energizing? Start there.
2. Define Your Focus for Each Doctrine:
   Once selected, identify a single focus behavior, challenge, or decision area for each doctrine. For example:
     - If you selected "Lead from the Front": How will you embody that in your home or workplace?
     - If you selected "Constant Directional Pressure": What goal or obstacle will you apply unrelenting progress toward?
     - If you selected "Fix Your Problem": What issue have you been tolerating instead of tackling?

3. Establish a Simple Tracking Format:
   Use a single notebook page (or the integrated page in this manual) to log:

   - Your three doctrines
   - The daily behaviors or actions aligned to each
   - Weekly assessments of progress, setbacks, and course corrections

4. Weekly Check-Ins:
   Every 7 days, conduct a Doctrine Debrief:
   - What moments tested your ability to live the doctrine?
   - Where did you apply it with strength?
   - Where did you abandon it—and why?
   - What insight emerged?
     Use these check-ins to recalibrate how you're applying the doctrine—don't assume understanding equals integration. It doesn't.

5. End-of-Month Review:
   At the close of each month, do a full review of your Doctrine Integration Cycle:
   - Rank your embodiment of each doctrine from 1–10.
   - Write a short reflection on how each doctrine changed your behavior, thinking, or results.
   - Decide whether to repeat the doctrine (for deeper embedding) or select new ones based on what your life demands next.

Field Notes Section:
Leave space each month to capture:

- Quotes, reminders, or phrases that reinforced the doctrine
- Observations from your environment that aligned (or conflicted) with your selected doctrines
- Real-world evidence that you're changing—these micro-wins are data points that track growth

Final Thought:

Mastery is built through layered exposure and intentional use. Most people give up too soon—assuming a doctrine "didn't work" after a few days of friction. But doctrine isn't meant to entertain you. It's meant to confront you, challenge your reflexes, and form a new pattern of operation in your life.

Three doctrines. Thirty days. One forged identity. Lock in. Begin now.

SECTION V — DAILY ENGAGEMENT SYSTEM

All growth is daily.

The gap between who you are and who you are becoming is only closed one day at a time. That's why this section exists. The Daily Engagement System is the living application of the entire Warriors & Winners framework—delivered through repeatable, high-impact routines that activate your ethos, refine your awareness, and shape your behavior where it matters most: in real time.

This is your field kit for daily execution.

Each morning, you'll return to a proven structure—built to prime your mind, ground your identity, and align your attention. It's not about perfection. It's about calibration. About showing up, recalibrating quickly, and moving forward with clarity and intent.

Each evening, you'll engage in a short but powerful reset—recording what you conquered, where you drifted, and how you'll return stronger tomorrow. These aren't boxes to check. They're touchpoints with your identity. Every day, you're not just measuring progress—you're forging the internal architecture that allows greatness to scale sustainably.

This system is intentionally undated. It's flexible enough to support you on your hardest days and robust enough to demand more from you when you're capable of it. Whether you use it 90 days in a row or come back after a setback, this format will meet you where you are—and push you toward who you're becoming.

Every decision counts. Every rep matters. Every day is a battlefield—and this is your daily command center.

Section 5.1: Daily Practice Pages

This is the most critical page in the entire manual. Because this is where identity is forged. Not in grand declarations or sweeping vision, but in the small, consistent, purposeful choices you make every single day.

This page is undated for a reason. It's meant to be used as a repeatable rhythm, not a one-off entry. The person you are becoming will not be built in a day—but you will either move closer to or further from that person today. This page helps you move closer, with clarity, power, and personal command.

Morning Setup: Your Strategic Entry Point into the Day

This morning section sets your posture, primes your nervous system, and initiates your mission for the day.

- Date
  Record the day. Not to mark time, but to own it.
- Wakeup Time / Sleep Quality
  Note what time you woke up and rate the quality of your rest (1–10). This helps you track energy patterns and take responsibility for recovery. Sleep is a weapon—track it like one.
- Breath Practice Log
  Record the number of rounds or minutes spent in breath work. Include any notes on how you feel. Even 2 minutes is enough to shift your baseline.
- One True Priority
  What one thing must happen today to move your mission forward? The rest is noise. Name the one true priority. Defend it.

- Intention Statement

  Write a clear intention for how you want to be today. Not just what you want to do—how you will show up. This is your inner calibration before outer execution.

- Doctrine of the Day

  Which Warrior & Winner doctrine will you embody today? Write the title and one sentence that translates it into behavior. Use this like a battle cry.

- Sacred Thing I Will Honor Today

  What sacred thing—one of your core values or convictions—will you deliberately protect, reinforce, or express today? If your life were on trial, would there be evidence of it?

- Warrior Question of the Day

  Each day, this manual will provide a deep, sharp question to force clarity. Write your answer with ruthless honesty. Then live in response to it.

Evening Reflection: Full Accountability at Day's End

This is the after-action review. The field report. The moment of truth.

- Summary of Actions Taken

  What did you actually do? Don't fluff this. List what was executed. Your output is your reflection.

- Resistance Faced & Response

  Where did you meet friction? Fatigue? Fear? Distraction? More importantly, how did you respond? This is where self-leadership grows.

- Micro-Win of the Day

  What small victory did you claim? Track it. Celebrate it. Stack these wins.

- Integrity Check (1–10 Scale)

  Did your actions align with your intentions? Rate yourself. Not to judge, but to calibrate. If the number is low, what specifically caused the misalignment?

- Noticing

  What stood out today? What did you see, sense, or feel that taught you

- something? This is your noticing log—train your eyes and instincts to get sharper daily.
- Where I Led, Where I Drifted

  What moment today revealed your leadership? What moment showed your drift? Write them both. These are the coordinates of your growth edge.
- Reset for Tomorrow

  One sentence. One commitment. One truth. What will you carry forward—and what will you leave behind? Set the next day's launchpad while the fire of this one still burns.

Final Instructions:

This page is your mirror. Your proving ground. Your recalibration tool. Use it every day. Not for perfection, but for precision. The goal is not to feel inspired—the goal is to be transformed.

And transformation requires truth.

This is where you tell it.

DAILY PRACTICE PAGE — MORNING SETUP

Date: _____
Wake Time: _____
Sleep Quality (1–10): _____

Breath Practice Log

Which breath technique did you use this morning (box, tactical or other)?

How long did you engage in focused breath work?
_____ minutes

How do you feel afterward?

One True Priority

What is the single most important thing you must move forward today?

Why is this priority non-negotiable?

Intention Statement

Write your intention for how you will move through today:

Doctrine of the Day

Which doctrine are you focusing on today?

What behavior will reflect this doctrine?

Sacred Thing I Will Honor Today

Choose one of your sacred things (e.g., Family, Faith, Purpose, Excellence, Service).

How will you honor it through your actions or attitude today?

Warrior Question of the Day

What is the question you must ask yourself to stay alert, aligned, and aggressive today?

How will this question shape your focus and decisions?

DAILY PRACTICE PAGE — EVENING REVIEW

Date: _____

Summary of Actions Taken

What did you do today that mattered?

Where did you win—no matter how small?

Resistance Faced & Response

What resistance showed up today—internal or external?

How did you respond?

What would you do differently next time?

Micro-Win of the Day

What is one moment you're proud of today?

Why does it matter?

Integrity Check

On a scale of 1 to 10, how aligned were your actions with your ethos today?
(1 = I drifted all day, 10 = I led with clarity and power)
Score: _____

What pulled you off track—if anything?

What got you back on?

Noticing

What did you observe about your mindset, body, behavior, or environment today?

Any signs, lessons, or insights you should carry forward?

Where I Led, Where I Drifted

Where did you take decisive, value-aligned action?

Where did you avoid, delay, or collapse?

Reset for Tomorrow

What needs to be reset, recalibrated, or recommitted to before tomorrow begins?

How will you prime yourself for a better day ahead?

Section 5.2: Weekly Tactical Review

This subsection is your built-in after-action review for the week. It is the tactical checkpoint where progress is measured, patterns are revealed, and corrections are made. In high-stakes environments, nothing is left to chance. This is where Warriors & Winners stop guessing about growth and start charting it.

You don't evolve by waiting for clarity. You evolve by pursuing it. This is the space where you review your doctrine alignment, precursor integration, and behavioral patterns. It's how you close the feedback loop—so that lessons don't get lost and mistakes don't get repeated.

You'll complete this every seventh day—same time, same rhythm. Make it a sacred appointment.

Progress Assessment
Start by looking at your stated goals, commitments, and intentions from the beginning of the week. What was completed? What wasn't? This isn't about shame or self-congratulation—it's about calibration. List the wins. Note the misses. Anchor into honesty.

Doctrine Mastery Log
Which doctrines did you focus on this week? Where did you apply them? Where did they fall off? Be specific. You're building pattern recognition. If a doctrine was weak in execution, ask: was it due to forgetting, resisting, or misapplying?

Precursor Integration Log
Which precursor was alive in you this week? Which one was neglected? Write about where you saw it show up—either by your deliberate action or in its absence. The more honest you are here, the more powerful your refinement becomes.

What Did I Conquer This Week?

Name one thing—large or small—that required your full focus, presence, or courage. This could be a conversation, a workout, a deadline, or a moment of restraint. Document it. This is your earned ground.

Where Did I Regress & Why?

Where did you drift, avoid, or shrink? Do not skip this. Failure only weakens you when it's hidden. What happened, why, and what will you do differently next time?

Reset Strategy

Based on what you've reviewed—what must change next week? What habits need reinforcement? What patterns must be disrupted? Write 1–3 shifts you will implement. This becomes your launchpad for the week ahead.

Final Note:

You don't master life by sprinting endlessly. You master it by stopping long enough to see what's working, what's not, and what must change. This is your chance. This is the pause that powers the next move.

SECTION VI — WEEKLY RHYTHM RESETS

If the days are your battleground, the weeks are your campaign.

This section is where you stop running blindly and start adjusting with precision. In CONQUER CULTURE, progress isn't left to guesswork. It's measured. Reviewed. Refined. And reset every seven days with intention and clarity.

This is your personal operations center.

Each week, you'll engage in two cycles—first, a Tactical Review, and then a Strategic Reset. The review allows you to extract wisdom from the week behind you: Where did you apply the doctrine? Where did you drift? What resistance did you face, and how did you respond? This is where you turn experience into insight.

Then, you'll step forward with deliberate targeting. You'll set micro-goals aligned with your broader objectives. You'll select doctrines to focus on. You'll identify potential obstacles, leadership opportunities, and pressure points. You'll move into the next week with a battle plan—not blind hope.

Without rhythm, even the most powerful system will collapse. Weekly Rhythm Resets give you structure, space, and sightlines. They're not just reflection tools. They are recalibration rituals.

If you don't lead your weeks, they will lead you. But when you do this with consistency, the gap between who you are and who you're becoming shrinks week by week—until that future self is standing right where you are.

Section 6.1: Weekly Tactical Review

Before any progress can be scaled, it must first be measured. And before momentum can be carried forward, the friction points must be named. That's the purpose of the Weekly Tactical Review—a built-in recalibration process that refines your growth, clarifies your drift, and re-engages your will.

At the end of each week, set aside time—quiet, focused, and uninterrupted—to walk yourself through the tactical review. You are not just filling in a worksheet. You are conducting a leadership audit of your own life.

Progress Assessment
Start by evaluating your execution. Did you follow through on the micro-goals you targeted this week? What was completed? What was missed? This is not a space for shame—it's a space for honesty. A Warrior & Winner doesn't avoid the truth; they seek it. Identify what moved forward, what stalled, and what patterns emerged.

Doctrine Mastery Log
Which doctrines did you apply this week? Where did they show up in your behavior? Where did they drift? Write down the moments you lived them and the ones where you left them behind. This is not theory—it's application. Every doctrine must become real in your daily actions, not just your intentions.

Precursor Integration Log
What precursor needed more attention this week? Did you operate with Prove It to Yourself? Did you Guard Your Thoughts under pressure? Did you Take Calculated Risks where needed? Log the precursor you trained most—and the one you ignored or resisted. Every precursor missed is a clue to the next week's opportunity.

What Did I Conquer This Week?
Name the wins. Big or small. You don't need applause—but you do need awareness. Where did you push past resistance? Where did you respond

differently? Where did you act like the man or woman you're becoming—not the one you used to be?

Where Did I Regress—& Why?
What triggered your drift this week? What environment, conversation, fatigue point, or distraction opened the door to compromise or retreat? Write it down without excuse. Identify the variables. Then build your strategy to neutralize them in the next round.

Reset Strategy
Now you choose how to reset. You don't need to rebuild from scratch. You recalibrate, adjust, and re-engage. What will you do differently next week? What will you reinforce? What needs to be eliminated? The review ends with forward movement—always.

Closing Charge
Most people skip the review. That's why most people never change. Warriors & Winners conduct tactical reviews not because it's easy—but because it sharpens their clarity, tunes their discipline, and locks in the lessons that others miss.

6.1 Weekly Tactical Review — The Rhythm Reset

Purpose: Clear the clutter, reflect with precision, recalibrate the system, and prepare for re-engagement. This is your built-in pattern interrupt—a strategic pause to reflect, refine, and reset the rhythm of performance, leadership, and personal integrity.

WEEKLY RHYTHM RESET

Week Ending: _____

Progress Assessment

What were my 3 most important objectives for the week?

Did I complete them? Why or why not?

What pattern helped me most this week?

What distracted or derailed me?

Doctrine Mastery Log

Which doctrine(s) did I focus on this week?

Doctrine 1: _____

Doctrine 2: _____

(Optional) Doctrine 3: _____

How did I apply each one?

Where did I fall short or default back to old patterns?

Precursor Integration Log

Which Precursor did I emphasize this week?

How did it shape my mindset or actions?

What resistance or insight surfaced?

What Did I Conquer This Week?

List 1–3 meaningful wins that reflect personal progress or power-in-motion.

Where Did I Regress & Why?

Identify the moments or behaviors that pulled you off course—and why they happened.

What part of my personal operating system is still compromised or needs reinforcement?

Reset Strategy

What one system, habit, or mindset must I reset or adjust immediately?

What doctrine, precursor, or daily ritual will I rely on to make that change stick?

What single decision will launch the week ahead with momentum and clarity?

Section 6.2: Weekly Targeting & Preparation

At the end of every week, before the next one begins, you recalibrate—not as a reset from failure, but as a deliberate repositioning of power. This section is where intention is weaponized. Warriors & Winners don't roll into the week reacting to noise. They aim first. They target what matters. And then they move with clarity and command.

Your weekly targeting process is the foundation of momentum.
Without it, even the most disciplined routines can fall prey to drift. With it, you begin every week already aligned with purpose, with friction reduced and priorities sharpened. This is not a passive review. It's tactical rehearsal. It's you stepping into the war room of your life, deciding what must happen, what cannot be allowed to happen, and how you'll respond to what may.

Micro-Goals for the Week

Every week begins with a question: What are the three most critical actions I must complete this week that would move me decisively toward my larger mission? These are not "to-do" list items. These are mission-milestones—small but strategically loaded targets that reinforce progress, confidence, and credibility with yourself.

Write them out. Speak them aloud. Then reverse-engineer how you'll hit them.

Each micro-goal should be:

- Aligned with your 90-day conquest
- Measurable and binary (complete or not complete)
- High leverage (it moves multiple needles at once)

You don't need 10. You need three. Hit them hard.

Doctrine Focus Selection

From your rotating doctrine cycle, select the one primary doctrine you will emphasize this week. Write it where you will see it daily. Think about it in your morning ritual. Use it as your lens for decisions, pressure moments, and reflection.

Ask:

- Where in my life does this doctrine need to live more fully?
- What would it look like to embody this doctrine this week under stress, not just in peace?
- How can I lead others by demonstrating it visibly?

Repetition without reflection is noise. But focused repetition becomes identity. That's what this section builds.

Schedule Design & Obstacle Planning

This part separates performers from dabblers. It's where you strategically control your calendar instead of letting others hijack it.

Use the following process:

- Build your week around your micro-goals and doctrine—not after everything else is booked.
- Identify anchor events: work, workouts, reflection, spiritual time, and family connection.
- Then map possible obstacles and derailments: interruptions, conflicts, patterns of drift.
- For each obstacle, write a pre-response. Train the reflex now, before it's needed.

Anticipation is a superpower. Predict the points of friction before they sabotage your execution.

Leadership Opportunity Map

This is where Warriors & Winners go beyond personal performance.

Each week, ask:

- Where will someone be watching how I lead?
- Who is within my influence that needs strength, guidance, or example?
- What opportunity exists to serve, mentor, protect, or elevate someone else?

This doesn't require a title. Leadership begins wherever you carry presence and responsibility.

Map 1–2 leadership moments this week and make them matter.

Weekly Targeting & Preparation is the difference between busy and built. Between performing well and leading powerfully. Between another week lost to drift—and one seized with conviction.

You are the architect of your calendar. You are the one responsible for how your energy is allocated, how your values show up in action, and how your vision is protected against the onslaught of distraction.

So draw the map. Set the targets. Plan the pressure points.
And then, move into the week like the warrior you've been becoming.

WEEKLY TARGETING & PREPARATION

Week Starting: _____

Micro-Goals for the Week

What are the three most important objectives I must achieve this week?

Why do these matter to me?

What is the one action each day that will move me toward each goal?

Doctrine Focus Selection

What doctrine(s) will I deliberately train and apply this week?

Doctrine 1: _____

Doctrine 2: _____

(Optional) Doctrine 3: _____

What situations or environments will be my training ground for each?

What does success look like in the application of each doctrine?

Schedule Design & Obstacle Planning

Where are the pressure points or environmental stressors in the week ahead?

What proactive decisions will I make now to reduce friction or distraction?

How will I maintain focus on what matters most when stress or urgency arise?

Leadership Opportunity Map

Where do I have the opportunity to lead this week—formally or informally?

How will I model clarity, courage, and consistency in these moments?

What is the highest standard I can set through my actions this week?

SECTION VII — SPECIAL OPERATIONS: HIGH-IMPACT DRILLS

This is the proving ground.

In every discipline, there are moments when theory gives way to test. When knowing must become doing. When what's been rehearsed must be executed under fire. That's what this section is for—training for those moments that don't come with warning. High-pressure. High consequence. High leverage.

Here, you'll find Special Operations—real-world simulations, personal edge drills, and identity-forging exercises that move beyond daily practices. These are not warmups. They're not reflective journaling prompts. They are pressure chambers, designed to compress time, reveal weakness, and harden capability.

You'll step into scenarios that test emotional control, decision-making speed, role conflict, and clarity under uncertainty. You'll train your ability to reset rapidly, to lead under fire, and to reinforce the sacred things that define your direction. These drills simulate the messiness of life and demand that you bring order through action.

You'll also work on sacred integration exercises—designed to draw you back to what matters when clarity fades. You'll write letters, interrogate mortality, and step into the future through guided self-dialogue. These exercises create the emotional leverage you need to remember why you fight, why you serve, and why you refuse to quit.

This section is not about balance. It's about extremes.

If the daily pages build habits, and the doctrine builds systems, these drills build nerve. They stretch your identity and set fire to the edges of your comfort zone. They bring you face to face with the question: when pressure hits, who shows up?

That answer—rehearsed here—will shape your real-world results.

Section 7.1: Situational Challenges & Simulations

Theory is only useful to the extent that it can be applied under pressure.

This section exists to create that pressure deliberately. Situational challenges and simulations are designed to stress-test your principles, activate your doctrine under fire, and reveal where you default when the stakes feel real.

Each challenge in this section invites you to do more than think—it invites you to act. You'll be required to write, rehearse, reflect, and recalibrate. The simulations are drawn from the high-consequence dynamics faced by Warriors & Winners in the real world—whether that be a negotiation, a leadership test, a moral failure, or a moment of emotional collapse.

Here's how to approach each simulation:

1. Create context — Set aside time and space where you can fully engage. Treat this like a live drill. No multitasking. No distractions.
2. Engage the challenge — Read the prompt. Step into the scene. Write, move, breathe, and decide as though the situation were real.
3. Debrief with precision — After completing each challenge, use the post-scenario questions to assess your instincts, breakdowns, insights, and adjustments.

These aren't hypotheticals. These are pressure tests—tools to simulate what it means to lead, decide, and act with clarity under tension. Warriors & Winners don't just train in theory. They rehearse stress. They pre-load clarity. And they condition response under fire. Each of these simulation drills is followed by journaling prompts so you can translate simulated challenge into real-world insight and future readiness.

Simulation 1: High-Pressure Decision Drill

Scenario: A team you're leading hits an unexpected obstacle. Time is short. Details are incomplete. There's risk either way. You must choose between two competing options.

Prompt: What doctrine do you consider when time, clarity, and certainty are not on your side?

Your Decision:

Why Did You Choose It?

What Was the Cost of Hesitation or Delay?

What Would You Do Differently With More Time?

Simulation 2: Failure Recovery Simulation

Scenario: You failed. You let someone down. Maybe you froze. Maybe you missed the mark. It's already happened—and now everyone's watching your next move.

Prompt: How do you recover and lead forward?

Describe the Failure Event:

Your Immediate Emotional Reaction:

What Did You Say or Do to Regain Ground?

Did You Overcorrect, Stay Centered, or Retreat?

What Doctrine Could Have Prevented It?

What Precursor Would Help You Recover Faster Next Time?

Simulation 3: Role Conflict Resolution

Scenario: You are pulled between duty and desire—between two sacred things or conflicting roles. A decision is required, and both paths have cost.

Prompt: How do you resolve the tension when both sides matter deeply?

What Two Roles Were in Conflict?

What Did Each Role Require of You?

What Decision Did You Make?

What Was the Justification?

Was the Cost Worth the Outcome?

How Will You Strengthen Clarity for Next Time?

Simulation 4: Lead from the Front Challenge

Scenario: You're asking others to act with courage, commitment, or clarity—but have you modeled it?

Prompt: Where do you need to step up first before you speak?

Who Are You Currently Leading or Influencing?

What Message Are You Sending With Your Actions?

What Action Would Align You Better With the Standard You're Asking Others to Uphold?

When Will You Take That Action? (Write the date & time)

Simulation 5: The 5-Minute Rule Reset Practice

Scenario: You're hit with a disappointment, setback, or insult. You get 5 minutes to respond emotionally. Then you must move on. Can you?

Prompt: Practice releasing emotional inertia and moving forward.

Describe the Triggering Event:

Emotional Response in First 5 Minutes:

Breath Practice or Reframe Used to Reset:

What Action Did You Take After the Reset?

Did You Maintain Your Integrity & Direction?

Summary

These five drills are designed to be repeatable. Revisit them monthly. Use them as part of your rhythm resets. Warriors & Winners do not wait for difficulty to test them—they simulate it, shape their response, and enter the world already conditioned to lead under pressure.

These drills are not hypotheticals. They are invitations. Use them regularly. Repeat them when circumstances change. Reflect with ruthless honesty. And when possible, engage them in the presence of someone you trust—a coach, a partner, a peer—who will not let you play small.

Because pressure reveals the truth. And Warriors & Winners are forged in nothing less.

Section 7.2: Sacred Things Reinforcement Exercises

At the core of CONQUER CULTURE lives a singular, unshakable truth: What is sacred must be protected.

Your Sacred Things—those people, values, principles, and callings that matter most—are the reason you fight, the source of your courage, and the fuel for your endurance.

But in the drift of life, we forget.
We get distracted.
We compromise.

This section exists to stop that from happening.

These exercises are designed to reconnect you to what's sacred. To keep it centered. To help you re-enter the battlefield of life with fire in your gut and clarity in your heart.

Do these drills quarterly, or anytime your motivation feels disconnected from your mission.

SACRED THING REINFORCEMENT EXERCISES

In a culture driven by noise, speed, and surface-level pursuits, remembering what matters most is a rebellious act. These exercises are not philosophical detours—they are recalibration drills designed to reinforce your sacred things. If you lose touch with what matters, you lose your direction. If you stay rooted in your sacred things, you can endure, overcome, and lead.

These pages are built to help you realign your thoughts, commitments, and identity with what you've named as sacred. Return to them as often as needed. Repetition will forge the clarity you need.

Exercise 1: Writing Your Legacy Letter

Prompt: If you were to write one letter that would be read by your children, spouse, closest allies, or students after you're gone—what would it say?

Objective: Clarify your values, legacy, and what you hope others carry forward from your life.

Instructions: Write from the heart. Speak as if this is the last message you will leave. Honor the people, principles, and moments that shaped you. Commit to what matters.

Legacy Letter:

Write your letter below:

Exercise 2: Interview with Your Future Self

Prompt: Imagine you're sitting across from yourself 20 years from now. This version of you has lived aligned with your sacred things, made courageous decisions, and honored your purpose. What would they tell you?

Objective: Connect with the version of yourself you are becoming. Gain clarity on who that person is—and how you must show up now to get there.

Instructions: Ask your future self questions. What did they struggle through? What are they most proud of? What advice do they have for you today?

Interview Dialogue:

Your Questions:

Future Self's Answers:

Exercise 3: "If I Had 30 Days" Decision Matrix

Prompt: If you were given only 30 days left to live—how would you live differently? Who would you reach out to? What would you let go of? What would you start today?

Objective: Bring urgency and perspective into your decision-making. Strip away the trivial and clarify the essential.

Instructions: Use the following matrix to audit your current commitments and habits through the lens of 30 days.

Reflection Matrix:

What I Would STOP Immediately:

What I Would START Immediately:

People I Would Reconnect or Reconcile With:

Habits I Would Double Down On:

Words I Need to Say While I Can:

Sacred Things I Would Build My Days Around:

Final Prompt:

How would your decisions today change if you lived with the clarity of these 30 days—every day?

Write your answer:

These exercises aren't meant to be completed once. They're recalibration tools—designed to return you to what matters most when life drifts, pressure builds, or you forget the "why" behind your work. Warriors & Winners don't wait to remember what's sacred. They live from it daily.

SECTION VIII — LONG-RANGE VISION & STRATEGIC MAPPING

Tactics win battles. Strategy wins wars.

Everything you've done up to this point has been about reclaiming daily discipline, rewriting your operating system, and stepping into clarity-driven action. But the goal was never just to win today. It was to build a future that's unmistakably yours—a life shaped by design, not drift.

This section is where you learn to do that with precision.

"Long-Range Vision & Strategic Mapping" is your command center. Here, you'll step above the daily fight and take a bird's eye view. You'll assess your trajectory, build out your conquest plans, and chart the milestones that will define the next phase of your evolution. This isn't about fantasy goals or vague aspirations—it's about architecting a future that aligns with your deepest values, your sacred things, and your current capacity.

In the 90-Day Conquest Plan, you'll choose a primary objective—something that will stretch your skills, test your commitment, and elevate your identity. You'll break it into phases, assign deadlines, and get brutally honest about the resources, relationships, and rhythms that either support or sabotage you.

In the Annual Leadership Calibration, you'll run a year-end audit. What did you conquer? Where did you fall short? What ground did you gain—and what did you abandon, intentionally or otherwise? From there, you'll begin mapping your next summit. This section ensures that each year of your life is lived with rising intention, built on the bedrock of clarity and the fire of consistent action.

A Warrior & Winner doesn't just survive the calendar—they dominate it.

This section teaches you how.

Section 8.1: 90-Day Conquest Plans

A Warrior & Winner never moves aimlessly. You do not drift. You direct.

The 90-Day Conquest Plan exists to give your focus a form and your fire a structure. It's where long-term vision meets tactical execution—where what you value becomes what you build.

This is not a dream journal. It's a war map.

Every 90-day cycle is a campaign. Each quarter, you select a specific, high-impact objective that aligns with your Sacred Things, stretches your capacity, and forces you to evolve. You'll then break that mission into executable milestones, identify your resources, build your support network, and create the conditions to win.

The process is detailed. It must be. Because if your plan lacks clarity, your execution will lack force. And force is what reshapes your reality.

Step One: Select Your Conquest Objective

Ask yourself:
What is the one thing, if accomplished in the next 90 days, that would radically shift your trajectory?

It could be physical (drop body fat, finish a race), professional (launch the project, double the revenue), relational (rebuild trust, set boundaries), or spiritual (daily practice, breakthrough clarity).

But it must be three things:
Meaningful. Measurable. Mobilizing.

Write your 90-Day Conquest Objective in one clear sentence. Declare it with conviction.

Step Two: Tactical Breakdown

Now reverse-engineer it. Break the 90-day span into three 30-day phases:

- Month 1 — Initiate: What must be done immediately to start with force?
- Month 2 — Expand: What systems, habits, or reps must be installed or repeated to lock in momentum?
- Month 3 — Execute: What must be finished, measured, or closed to cross the finish line?

List the actions, events, or habits that will define each month. Treat each as a micro-campaign.

Step Three: Milestone Mapping

Set three critical checkpoints—milestones that prove you're progressing:

1. Milestone 1 (Day 30): Early validation—you're moving.
2. Milestone 2 (Day 60): Mid-course correction—tighten, double down, or pivot.
3. Milestone 3 (Day 90): Finish line—complete, review, recalibrate.

Each milestone must include one measurable outcome and one reflection prompt:

- What did I conquer?
- Where did I resist?
- What must change to keep momentum?

Step Four: Resource & Relationship Mapping

No Warrior fights alone. Even the fiercest independent fighter requires training, feedback, and accountability.

List the resources you need to win—books, tools, finances, systems, training. Then list the relationships that will either help or hinder your progress—mentors, partners, allies, enemies.

Build your environment to support the man you're becoming—not the one you're leaving behind.

Step Five: Begin the Conquest

On Day 1 of your plan, write a one-paragraph Personal Conquest Declaration. This is your stake in the ground. Your activation statement. Speak to the mission, the reason behind it, and the man who will emerge on the other side.

Sign it. Date it. Start.

Then execute.
One rep. One decision. One battle at a time.

90-DAY CONQUEST PLAN

Section 8.1 — Tactical Mapping Template
Define. Break down. Execute. Adjust. Win.

CONQUEST TITLE (Name Your Mission)

A compelling name to activate identity and urgency.

START DATE: _____ TARGET DATE: _____

OBJECTIVE CLARIFICATION

What is the singular outcome I will achieve in the next 90 days?
Write your objective in clear, measurable, and time-bound terms.

Why does this matter deeply to me?
Tie this goal to your Sacred Things, your ethos, or your long-term trajectory.

TACTICAL BREAKDOWN

Break your conquest into 3 sequential Mission Blocks, each 30 days long. Each block should build toward the final outcome with increasing intensity.

MISSION BLOCK 1 — Weeks 1–4

Focus: _____

Tactics & Milestones:

MISSION BLOCK 2 — Weeks 5–8

Focus: _____

Tactics & Milestones:

MISSION BLOCK 3 — Weeks 9–12

Focus: _____

Tactics & Milestones:

WEEKLY MICRO-TARGETS

Each week, you'll define and hit at least one key target tied to your larger block milestone. Use this space to identify 4 priority targets per block.

Block 1 – Priority Weekly Targets

1.
2.
3.
4.

Block 2 – Priority Weekly Targets

1.
2.
3.
4.

Block 3 – Priority Weekly Targets

1.
2.
3.
4.

RESOURCES & RELATIONSHIPS

Who and what must be involved to help me succeed?
Consider training, mentorship, spiritual counsel, tools, accountability, etc.

What sacrifices must I make to win?

OBSTACLES & ADJUSTMENTS

What internal resistance do I anticipate?

What external disruptions might derail me?

What will I do when I hit resistance?
Pre-decide how you will recalibrate.

IDENTITY & INTEGRITY

What identity do I need to embody to complete this mission?

What would full integrity look like across these 90 days?

Section 8.2: Annual Leadership Calibration

At the end of every campaign season, true Warriors & Winners do not just celebrate. They calibrate.

This section is your end-of-year command post—a time to step off the battlefield, survey what has been conquered, what has been left behind, and what mountain now calls you forward. It's not about guilt. It's not about hype. It's about clear-eyed reflection and elite-level preparation.

Leadership is not maintained by effort alone—it must be recalibrated. Because what got you here won't get you there.

The Annual Leadership Calibration is your opportunity to consolidate gains, confront drift, and prepare with precision for the next summit. If done correctly, this practice will not only highlight where you've grown—it will make clear where you must evolve next.

Step One: Year-End Audit

Begin by looking back—without emotion, without excuse.

Answer these core calibration prompts:

- What were my top three wins this year?
- What values did I honor most consistently?
- Where did I grow the most as a man? As a leader?
- What goal did I pursue that no longer aligns—and why?
- What pain or pressure revealed something vital about who I am?

Document these answers with depth. Don't rush. Let clarity come through ruthless honesty.

Step Two: Conquered Territory

Next, take inventory of what you claimed this year. What have you now built, mastered, overcome, or initiated that didn't exist at this level last year?

- What systems now run without friction?
- What relationships deepened or were redeemed?
- What personal patterns or fears were finally broken?
- What physical, spiritual, or emotional edge did you sharpen?

These are your victories. Name them. Own them. Solidify them.

Now write one paragraph summarizing the Territory You Have Conquered. Read it out loud. Let it land.

Step Three: Abandoned Ground

Now confront the spaces where you fell short—not with shame, but with responsibility.

- What habits collapsed when pressure hit?
- What goals were quietly abandoned?
- What relationships were neglected or mismanaged?
- What beliefs or behaviors repeatedly pulled you off course?

These are not failures. They are intelligence. They tell you where to fortify, where to reset, and what must be re-engaged with purpose.

Write your Abandoned Ground Acknowledgment in one paragraph. Call out what you left behind—and what you will now reclaim.

Step Four: Planning the Next Summit

Now lift your eyes.

What mountain is next? What territory must be taken to become the next version of you? Think beyond comfort, beyond repetition. Think transformation.

- What one outcome would radically evolve your identity, capacity, or leadership?
- What would make 12 months from now undeniably different?
- What sacred thing are you now called to protect, promote, or pursue?

Define your next summit in one clear sentence. Then identify your three Preparation Priorities—the first moves that must be made to establish traction in Q1.

Final Leadership Statement

Close this process by writing your Leadership Calibration Statement—a declaration of the man you are becoming, the life you are building, and the standard you now uphold.

Sign it. Date it. Mark the transition.

You've earned the right to reflect—but you've also accepted the responsibility to rise. And now, a new campaign begins.

ANNUAL LEADERSHIP CALIBRATION

Section 8.2 — Year-End Audit & Summit Design

What did you conquer? What did you abandon? What will you build next?

YEAR-END STRATEGIC REVIEW

What was my greatest conquest this year?

Write the story. Include what made it significant and how you changed.

What doctrine or principle best defined my year?

Where did I lead? Where did I lag?

Be honest. Leadership is revealed in both action and avoidance.

What was my biggest personal growth moment this year?
What cracked open? What refined you?

Where did I drift from my Ethos or Sacred Things?

And what were the consequences?

TERRITORY MAP

Conquered Ground

List the areas of your life where you advanced, built, or gained ground.

Abandoned Ground

List the areas where you withdrew, lost discipline, or failed to act.

Neutral Ground

Where did you maintain but not grow?

What will I reclaim, reinforce, or release next year?

LEADERSHIP IMPACT REPORT

Who did I influence this year and how?

Leadership isn't only what you build—it's who you impact.

How did I serve? Where did I fall short?

Where did I model the Conquer Culture identity most clearly?

STRATEGIC VISION — THE NEXT SUMMIT

What is the next summit I must pursue?
It must be worthy of the next version of you.

What identity must I become to reach that summit?

What doctrine will be my guidepost for the year ahead?

What is my ONE WORD for the year?
Let it define your focus, filter, and firepower.

_____

What is my Year's Final Declaration?
Write one sentence that captures your intent, your posture, and your purpose heading into the next chapter of life.

SECTION IX — CLOSING COMMANDS: LIVING THE CODE

This is where the training ends—but the transformation begins.

You've moved through doctrine, integrated discipline, identified your sacred things, and installed a system that can serve you for life. But before you close this manual, before you lay it down and return to your world, there is one final, critical step: lock it in.

This section exists to mark the transition from student to practitioner. From learner to leader. From seeker to system. Warriors & Winners don't just know the path—they walk it daily, visibly, powerfully. And that's what these closing commands are designed to do: give you a place to recommit, to reflect, and to formalize the internal shift that's already underway.

You'll begin by issuing yourself final orders—reminders of what this journey has awakened and where it now calls you to lead. You'll reflect through two letters: one to the person you were when you began, and one from the future self who will carry this system forward. And finally, you'll sign a Commitment Statement—not just as a ceremonial close, but as a physical, dated record of who you chose to become and what you vowed to embody.

You've done the work. You've confronted the truth. You've stepped into the forge and emerged sharper, stronger, and more aligned. Now it's time to lead.

Because a Warrior & Winner doesn't just carry the code.

He becomes it.

Section 9.1: Your Final Orders

Recommit to the Ethos • Lead, Serve, Sharpen • Advance the Culture

You've made it to the final section—not because this work is finished, but because you are now ready to take command of what comes next.

This is not a conclusion. It's a commissioning.

The Warrior & Winner doesn't walk away from the fire of discipline, the furnace of self-leadership, or the battlefield of belief. He moves forward—armed with a forged identity, a field-tested system, and a purpose sharp enough to cut through every distraction life throws at him.

Your orders are not complicated—but they are comprehensive. They are meant to reorient you back to mission, to purpose, and to presence. Read them slowly. Read them often. And when clarity wavers, come back here to reset.

1. Recommit to the Ethos

Your Ethos is not a poetic phrase—it is a code you live by. The time to recommit is now.

Re-read your Sacred Things Inventory. Review your Ethos statement. Reflect on your defining beliefs, your deepest values, and the identity you've chosen to claim.

Say it out loud:
"This is who I am. This is who I serve. This is how I lead."

Your Ethos must be written on more than just the page. It must be etched into your behavior—visible to those you lead and unmistakable to the man in the mirror. Warriors & Winners do not wander. They live aligned.

2. Lead, Serve, Sharpen

You were not built to conquer only for yourself.
Leadership means leverage—multiplying impact by serving those around you.

- Where are you leading with integrity?
- Who are you sharpening through your presence, your discipline, your example?
- What environments are elevated simply because you enter them with clarity and strength?

Service is not weakness. It is legacy. When you lead others by embodying the Ethos, you give them permission to rise.

And when you sharpen others, you stay sharp yourself.

So teach what you know. Live what you teach. Carry the weight others can't. And remind those around you what it looks like to be forged through fire and focused on impact.

3. Advance the Culture

The final charge is simple: advance the CONQUER CULTURE.

This means two things:

First, never retreat to the man you used to be. That version of you is gone. You've trained your mind, hardened your resolve, confronted the shadows, and designed a new path. Stay on it. Keep pressing forward. Refuse to settle.

Second, become a multiplier. This culture spreads through embodiment. Not marketing. Not memes. Movement. When people see the way you speak, show up, train, lead, and recover—they'll feel something shift.

That's what this world needs.
Men who move with certainty.
Men who protect what's sacred.
Men who know what matters and live like it.

You are no longer in training.

You are operating. Executing. Leading.

So, write your Final Orders down in your own words. Place them where you can see them. Revisit them weekly.

And remember: this manual doesn't close.

It gets carried forward.

Section 9.2: Field Manual Commitment Statement

This manual was not written to entertain you.

It was written to awaken something in you—to demand a deeper level of ownership over your life, your choices, and your impact. It's a call to full-spectrum responsibility. A declaration that from this point forward, you will no longer drift through your days, outsource your power, or live below your calling.

This commitment is not to me.
It's not to a program, a brand, or a fleeting sense of motivation.

It is to yourself.

The version of you who wakes up with clarity, executes with discipline, leads with conviction, and lives with deep satisfaction is not a myth or a fantasy. He is real—and he is built through consistency, courage, and personal integrity. He is built by living out the truths, disciplines, and practices contained in this manual. Day by day. Moment by moment. Rep by rep.

You've been given the system. The principles. The map.

Now comes the vow to live it.

The Warrior & Winner Commitment

I hereby commit to living the Warrior & Winner ethos to the best of my ability each day.

I accept that perfection is not required—only full engagement.

I will lead from the front, guard my sacred things, and embody the doctrines I've chosen to live by.

I understand that this journey is not about hype, but about habit. Not about intensity alone, but consistency over time.

I commit to reviewing, refining, and recalibrating my operating system as I grow.

I will act.

I will serve.

I will lead.

I will conquer.

Name: _____

Signature: _____

Date: _____

Tape this to your mirror. Put it in your wallet. Tattoo it on your calendar. Whatever it takes—this is your line in the sand.

You are not the same man who started this journey.
And you are not going back.

ABOUT THE AUTHOR

CJ Kirk is a warrior, a builder, and a system designer. As Deputy Chief Instructor of Krav Maga Worldwide, Founder of Krav Maga Houston, and creator of the Courage Coaching Certification, he has spent decades training people to take command of their lives under pressure. He is also the Founder of Instructive Tactical Concepts and the Editor-in-Chief of Kravology. Based in Houston, Texas, he lives with his wife and five children.

But his credentials were earned, not given. After surviving an armed robbery, CJ's life took a decisive turn. He chose to confront chaos—not just physically, but mentally and spiritually—and that decision became the foundation for a life spent developing and teaching others how to do the same.

This manual is the tactical extension of the CONQUER CULTURE movement. Where the book casts vision and frames doctrine, the Warriors & Winners Field Manual demands application. It is where theory becomes action and identity becomes behavior. Built to be used, not just read, this manual will help you forge new instincts, refine daily execution, and build alignment between your beliefs and behavior—under pressure, in the real world.

Printed in Dunstable, United Kingdom